NEW Spirals



# Soulmates

Bill Ridgway

Published in 2004 by:
Nelson Thornes Ltd
Delta Place
27 Bath Road
CHELTENHAM
GL53 7TH
United Kingdom

04 05 06 07 08 / 10 9 8 7 6 5 4 3 2 1

A catalogue record for this book is available from the British Library

ISBN 0 7487 9000 4

Cover illustration by Jim Eldridge
Page make-up by Tech-Set, Gateshead

Printed in Croatia by Zrinski

# 1

No one can see Jo. Only me. I saw her twice that day. She came into the kitchen when I was getting ready for college. I saw her again at the end of the morning.

The first time she said nothing. She just stood by the door smiling her odd smile. She always smiled like that when something bad was going to happen.

The other time she tried to speak to me. No words came. That happens sometimes. At other times I can hear every word. She sounds just like me.

I see Jo a lot. I usually see her when there's a problem. I've learnt to trust her, but we fall out from time to time. She can turn up anywhere. On the stairs. In the bathroom. In the park. At college.
I never know.

I've even seen her in lectures. Once she was sitting next to the tutor. She made me smile, and I had to look down. The other time she was next to me. I got a funny look for turning round to speak to her.

It was no use trying to explain. No one would believe me. If she speaks, I'm the only one who can hear what she says. And that can make things hard at times.

On this day I knew something bad was going to happen. I could tell by the look on Jo's face. A sad sort of look that broke through her smile.

I stayed behind until the tutor and the group had gone. Just the two of us were in the room. Jo and me.

'What is it?' I said. 'Tell me.'

Her lips moved.

'I can't hear you,' I said. 'Why don't you say something?'

As I was speaking the tutor came back into the room.

'Who was that you were talking to, Debbie?' she asked.

'Talking? Me?'

'You were talking to someone over by the cupboard.'

'There's nobody in the cupboard,' I joked. 'I was just thinking out loud.'

She gave me a funny look. 'I knew someone who talked to himself. He ended up in a cage.'

'I'm sorry to hear that, Miss. Was he a boyfriend or something?'

'No. He was a budgie. Now, Debbie, if I were you I'd get off home.'

I was angry at Jo. I wanted to give her a piece of my mind. She was just going through the door. I followed her out.

But by then she'd turned a corner and vanished into thin air.

# 2

I always got the number 72 bus home from college. It ran past our house. None of the others used it. I lived a long way away and they don't live near me.

I used buses all the time. My mum never learnt to drive and my dad worked away a lot. I liked double-deckers best. I always sat on the top deck. From there you can see the world go by.

Number 72 buses were always single-deckers. So I was surprised when a red double-decker pulled up at the stop. I'd just put my leg on the step when I stopped. Jo was in my way. She was standing next to the driver, but he didn't know.

He must have been new. I'd never seen him before. He gave me an angry look. 'I haven't got all day. Are you getting on or not?'

This time Jo found her voice. 'No,' she said. 'You're not getting on. You're catching the next bus.'

'Don't be stupid, Jo. That's another hour.'

The words just came out. The driver gave me an odd look. 'What's another hour? And who's Jo?'

'Until the next bus,' I said. 'And Jo's a – . It doesn't matter.'

'Look, I haven't got all day. Are you getting on or not?'

'You're not,' Jo cried. 'Catch the next bus or walk home.'

'Thanks a lot, Jo,' I said.

'Jo? I can't see no Jo. I think you're mad,' said the driver, and drove off.

I watched Jo wave to me from the back seat. There were just two of them on the bus. Jo and the driver. It began to drizzle.

I didn't want to hang about for an hour, so I set off on foot. After a few minutes two police cars flew past. Then an ambulance. There must have been an accident.

My blood ran cold. I could hear Jo's voice ringing in my head. I began to run down the road. In the distance I could see police lights winking. As I drew near I saw what had happened.

There was a low bridge across the road. The double-decker had hit the bridge. The top of the bus was a wreck. They'd sent a double-decker by mistake. It wouldn't go under.

The driver was new on that road. By the time he'd braked it was too late. I saw him by the side of the road. He was in shock. One of the ambulance men sat with him.

I always went on the top deck. If it hadn't been for Jo I'd be dead.

# 3

I didn't see Jo for some time. Then she turned up in the lecture room. She was sitting next to me, smiling. She was out for fun, like the time before. Without thinking, I whispered, 'What are you doing here?'

I could feel eyes on me, and looked up.

'You'd better get on with your assignment, Debbie, said the tutor coldly. 'It's got to be in next week.'

I could feel myself go red. At the end of the session one of the lads came up to me.

'You should go on the stage,' he said.

I asked him what he meant.

'You should be a comic. Talking to an empty seat. You were a real laugh.'

I didn't think it was funny. I could see Jo by the window. She was enjoying herself. I gave her an angry look and she faded away. She was always getting me in scrapes. I could do without it.

I decided to change the subject. 'Didn't Mr Thomas tell us to go to his room this lunch break?' I asked. 'About the trip?'

'That's right. One o'clock.'

'I shall have to go,' I said. 'I have things to do.'

As I went, he called after me, 'Don't forget – get a job on TV. You'll be a hit.'

The trip was that Friday. We all got on the mini-bus. It was a bit cramped. Mr Thomas called our names and told us we were going up the motorway and into the hills. We were going to do a long walk and make notes on the things we saw.

We set off in sunshine. But as we went up the motorway the clouds started to come over. Drops of rain hit the screen. We went through patches of mist.

At last we saw the hills. They were very faint. Mr Thomas drew off the road and stopped the mini-bus.

'We're staying for an hour. You can eat your lunch and get a drink at the café. I want you all back at the bus in one hour. Then we can go for a nice long walk.'

Everyone gave a moan and got off. I was the last to leave. As I turned to shut the door I saw Jo. She was sitting in the driving seat.

She smiled at me. One of those sad smiles that chilled my blood.

# 4

It was drizzling as we set off. We wore plastic macs to keep dry. We had maps and food and drink in our back-packs.

The path was rough and full of stones. We were all joking at first. But we grew quiet as we walked on. As we climbed higher there was a faint mist. The tutor told us to stick together. 'Don't hang about,' he said. 'Stay on the path.'

The mist got thicker. A big rock loomed up. Someone was sitting on it. Someone in a red mac like mine. It was Jo. As we got up to the rock she held up her hand. She didn't speak, just held up her hand like a policeman.

'If it gets much worse we'll have to go back,' Mr Thomas was saying. 'Keep together. The path starts to go down soon. It'll be clear down below.'

I heard his voice fading. Everyone melted into the mist. I began to follow them but Jo blocked the path.

'Go back, Debbie.'

'Is this one of your jokes?' I said.

'There's no joke. Go back down. Go the way you came.'

'What about the others?'

But Jo had faded, and I was left on my own. I didn't know what to do. Should I go on and tell them or go back? Jo was never wrong. She might joke, but she always looked after me. The mist was getting thicker all the time. I wasn't sure I could find my way back.

I decided to tell the others. I set off after them. I hadn't taken more than ten steps when the path forked. Which way had they gone? I began to panic. I gave a shout but the mist swallowed up my voice.

I began to shiver. It was then I saw a red shape in the mist and Jo began to appear again.

'I'm lost, Jo,' I said.

'I know.'

'What am I going to do?'

She gave a smile. One of her warm smiles. She waved me to go to her. She seemed to float over the rocks. I followed her as well as I could. The path seemed longer than it was on the way up.
I tripped over stones. Everything was grey.

'It's not far now,' Jo said.

The mist began to clear. Far below I could see the mini-bus and the café. I looked back. I'd been walking only a few steps from a cliff face. I could have fallen. Jo had kept me safe. I followed her down and sat by the bus.

What had happened to the others? I began to worry. They shouldn't have gone on. Maybe they were lost in the mist. Maybe they were in danger.

As I sat I heard a phone ringing. There was a mobile on the roof of the mini-bus. It was the same as my mobile. The same name, the same colour. But it wasn't mine. I'd left mine at home. I'd been in a rush and forgotten it.

I put it to my ear. 'Hello?'

A voice at the other end said: 'This is Mountain Rescue. We've had a call from someone called Jo. About a college party lost in the hills. Are you Jo?'

Jo was leaning by the bus door. I looked across at her and shook my head. 'No. I'm not Jo. But I know the party. I've got a map of their route. I can show you the path they've taken.'

I told them where I was. The voice on the line said: 'Is Jo with you at the moment?'.

I looked around. Jo was no longer there. 'No,' I said. 'She seems to have vanished.'

# 5

How did Jo phone? I didn't know, but it was a good job she had. I found out later that Mr Thomas had tried to use his mobile. The signal wouldn't work in the hills. They'd got stuck in the fog. The rescue team had got them down. If I'd been with them I'd have got down too. Safe and sound. But Jo was taking no chances.

I didn't feel well for some days after that. I had a cold and sore throat. Mum kept me off lectures for a week. She was at work. The house was empty. I was hoping Jo might turn up to keep me company. But she never came.

By Friday I was fed up. I'd surfed the net. I'd read the mags. I'd done the crosswords. It was my friend's birthday. I'd got a card so I thought I'd send it now.

I looked around for a stamp. Mum kept them in a box with the bills and other papers. The box was always locked. She kept the key. But not that day. She must have forgotten. I could see the key on the shelf.

I put the box on the table and opened the lid. The inside was split into parts, some big, some small. I tried the smallest part first. I pulled out some postcards and a tin of paper clips. But no stamps.

I tried another part. That had some old letters in it. I didn't think she'd keep stamps in the big parts, but I slipped my hand inside just in case. Instead of stamps I pulled out a big brown envelope. On it two words were printed.

Two words that made me forget about stamps. Forget about everything. I stared at the envelope and the words written there.

Then I opened it.

# 6

The words on the envelope said ADOPTION PAPERS. I didn't know why the envelope was in the box. I was an only child. There were just the three of us: Mum, Dad and me. The papers in the envelope could only be about me.

My hands were shaking as I took out the papers. My name was at the top, and my date of birth. I began to read.

It didn't take me long to get to the end. I put the papers back in the envelope. I put the envelope back in the box and locked it. Then Jo appeared.

She was sitting at the end of the table. She wasn't speaking. She just sat there, looking hard at me.

'It's bad news, Jo,' I said.

She gave a little nod.

'I don't know what to do,' I said. 'It's the worst shock I've ever had.'

Jo looked through the window, then back at me. She said, 'It's a good job you found out. Don't worry.'

'But what do I do?'

'You must tell them,' Jo said. 'Tell them what you found.'

I heard the key in the door. Mum was back. I waited for her to come into the kitchen. 'And what have you been doing with yourself all day?' she asked.

'I've written a birthday card,' I said. 'I looked in the box for a stamp but I couldn't find one.'

She looked worried. 'You looked in the box? The box is locked.'

I held up the key. 'You left it behind,' I said. I looked at Jo. She smiled and nodded.

'Tell her what you found,' she said. 'Tell her you want to meet your real mother.'

'Don't worry, Jo. I'll tell her.'

Mum looked hard at me. 'Stop playing these silly games, Debbie. Talking to yourself. I thought you'd got over all that.'

I didn't answer. What was the point? 'I found some papers in an envelope,' I said. 'Adoption papers. Why didn't you tell me the truth? You aren't my real mother, are you?'

She turned pale and sat down. 'I was going to tell you, Debbie. I was waiting for the right time. We were worried, your Dad and me. Worried what you might think.'

'You should have told me before,' I shouted, in tears. 'I have a right to know.'

'It wasn't as easy as that,' she said. 'We've always been worried about you, Debbie. Ever since you were little. All this talking to yourself. Talking to someone who isn't there. It's been going on for years. At first we thought it was just a kid's make-believe friend. But it's never stopped. We wanted you to get well before you were told. We didn't want to give you a shock.'

'It's too late for that,' I said. 'I've already had one. And you're wrong. I keep trying to tell you. I've never made things up. I *do* see someone. Her name is Jo. I see her with my own two eyes. And I hear her speak. She looks like me. She acts like me. She wears the same clothes. And she's here now. In this room. Sitting at this table.'

I pointed. But as I pointed I began to see the cupboard through Jo's body as she melted into the air. I turned to Mum. 'Jo's going now, but she'll be back. She says I should meet my mother. My real mother.'

# 7

Jo had always been there to keep me from danger. Now she seemed to want to advise me too. That's what I thought as I tried to find out who my real mother was. Jo wanted me to find out. She wanted me to know.

In some ways I felt upset. Mum and Dad had always been good to me. I had my own room. They'd given me love as well as things. If they'd been my real parents they couldn't have treated me better. I felt I was letting them down.

But I'd always trusted Jo. We were like two peas in a pod. She seemed to know what I was thinking. You might think of her as a ghost. I suppose she was, in a way. But she was more than that. It was as if we were two parts of one person.

I had meetings with different people. Sometimes I went on my own. At other times Mum and Dad came with me. A woman asked me a lot of questions. Was I sure I wanted to find out about my real mother and father? Did I know it might make things hard for me? For everyone? Did I see myself moving out of the only home I'd ever known to live with someone I couldn't remember? Nothing was simple.

Then one day a letter came. It had my name on the envelope. I knew what it was. Even so, my hands shook as I opened it. I took out a sheet of paper and read the name and address on the top. There was a phone number too.

I went up to my room and locked the door. I switched on my mobile. I watched the buttons light up. I rang the number.

I waited.

A woman's voice came down the line.

'It's me,' I said. 'Debbie. Hello, Mum.'

# 8

I took the bus to a part of the city I'd never been to before. There was nobody on the top deck. My mouth was dry. My inside seemed to be tied in a knot. I wished I'd never opened the box. Never set eyes on that envelope. I'd had a good life. Now it was all going to change.

The woman who'd brought me up had been like a real mother to me. She'd always done her best. She'd even paid for me to see doctors. She'd thought I was speaking to someone who wasn't there. She'd thought I was going mad.

The doctors had given me pills. I'd thrown them away. I wasn't mad. Jo was real to me. She'd always been real to me. Ever since I was little. She'd told me not to go on a swing. I did what she said. Later, the chain snapped. She'd got older as I grew older. And now she was sitting by my side.

'Don't be scared,' she said.

'I'm not.'

'You are. I can feel you shaking.'

'It's cold. The cold always makes me shake.'

'You can't fool me,' Jo said as the bus stopped to pick up some people. 'Now you'd better shut up. You don't want them to see you talking to yourself again.'

'Well you shut up too,' I told her, and she laughed.

It was a long ride. I got off the bus outside a block of flats. There was no one about. I didn't like the place. It was full of junk and litter. There was graffiti all over the walls.

Jo was by my side. I felt safer with her there. I looked at the address I'd been given. Then I looked at the flats. Floor 5. That's what it said.

Jo was standing in a doorway. 'Come on, Debbie. I'll be with you.'

# 9

But when I knocked at the door she was nowhere to be seen. My heart was pounding. I waited. The passage was empty. There was no one about.

Then the door opened and a woman stood there. 'Debbie?'

I nodded. I didn't know what to say. What to think. For the first time I was speaking to my real mother, and I was lost for words.

She put her arms around me and gave me a hug. 'After all this time,' she was saying. 'I never thought I'd see you again.'

We dried our eyes and closed the door behind us. Jo was already in the room. She was sitting in a chair, smiling. Not the kind of smile she'd smiled before. She was smiling as if she was pleased for me. Pleased for both of us.

Mum went to make a cup of tea. 'We've got plenty to talk about,' she said. 'Years to catch up on. I never forgot you, Debbie. Not for a day.'

I looked through the window. Far below, the cars sped along the road. I could look out over our city and see the hills far away. Jo didn't say anything. I didn't speak to her. I didn't want my new-found Mum to find me talking to someone who wasn't there. I didn't want her to think I was mad.

'Here we are, Debbie.' She put the tray down. 'Help yourself to sugar.'

'I don't take sugar.'

'Neither do I. It must run in the family.'

I left her to do most of the talking. She said: 'I suppose you want to know how you came to be adopted. You must think I'm very bad, giving you up to somebody else.'

'I just want to know,' I said.

'It wasn't easy. I should never have done it. I know that now. At the time it seemed the right thing to do.'

Jo came to sit by me on the armchair. I forgot myself and moved the plate of biscuits so she could have one. My mother looked at me. 'Don't you like biscuits, Debbie? I got them in for you.'

‘Oh, yes,’ I said. ‘I was just passing them to- ‘ I stopped. ‘I’m just on edge. I always do silly things when I’m edgy.’

‘That’s okay, Debbie. I’m just the same. I’m a bag of nerves inside. You wouldn’t believe how hard it is for me. But I’m going to tell you what happened. I’m going to tell you everything.’

# 10

‘I had you when I was very young, Debbie. I’d just left school. I had a boyfriend. When I told him I was going to have a baby he didn’t want to know. He was only 18 himself. I never saw him after that. He never came to see how I was. He never even came to the hospital.

‘When you were on the way, I didn’t know what to do. Dad had left home and Mum had another man. I didn’t get on with him, so I left. I got a flat and a job. It didn’t pay much, but I made out.

‘Then you came along. It was the last straw. I couldn’t cope. There was no one to help. I was on my own in a poky little flat. Every day I was in tears.

‘Then this woman came. She was from the council. She looked at the flat. She said it needed a good clean. I told her I couldn’t cope. She asked if I’d thought of having my baby adopted.

Maybe I shouldn’t have said yes. I know how you must feel. First your father didn’t want you. Then I sent you for adoption. All I can say is I did it for the best. I did it to give you a better life. If I had my time over again I would have kept you. Of course I would. But I’d only just left school. I was mixed up.

'All these years I've wanted to get in touch. But I didn't want to upset you. I wanted you to be happy with your new parents. Not like me. My life has been a mess. I've been married twice. Nothing has worked out. So now there's just me. Are you still glad you came?'

What could I say? It was too much to take in at one go. I thought of the home I'd left. The good times. My real mother was thin and jumpy. Her hair needed doing. She'd let the flat go. Herself, too.

'Tell her you're glad,' Jo said.

I'd forgotten about Jo for the moment. She was no longer sitting by me. She was standing by my mother.

'Yes,' I said. 'I'm glad I came. Of course I am.'

My mother looked up. There were tears in her eyes. 'I'm glad too, Debbie.' She went quiet. Then she said, 'You might as well know the rest. I'll tell you something else that upset me when you were born. Something awful.'

I wondered what she was going to say. 'What?' I asked.

'You had a twin. She only lived a few hours. I was going to call her Josephine. You were Debbie, and she was Jo.'

I looked at Jo. She'd been with me since I was little. She'd kept me from danger. She'd helped me in all kinds of ways. At last I knew who she was. Jo was no ghost.

No. She was my sister.

# 11

Now I've left college and I'm working. I decided to stay with my adoptive parents. After all, they were the only family I'd ever known. It might seem hard to say so, but it was all for the best.

I still see my real mother. I call around most weekends. We go shopping. We go on day trips together. She's more like an older sister to me.

I think seeing me again has been good for her. Her flat is smart. She looks after herself once more. I'm glad. I never wanted to upset her.

Jo still turns up when there's a problem. Or when things get hard. I've learnt not to speak to her when people are about. It only makes problems. I don't want people to think I'm mad.

I wouldn't blame them. They say only mad people talk to someone who isn't there. And I'm the only one who can see Jo.

I thought I'd tell my real mother about her. Then I changed my mind. Things are best left as they are. She wouldn't believe me anyway. She'd think I wasn't all there too. How could I explain Jo to her? I can't even explain her to myself.

Jo doesn't worry me, ghost or not. She never has. She's my other half. My twin sister. My best friend. My soulmate.

No matter what, I know she'll always be around.